SCHOOLS SERVICE

Methuen Children's Books

The Family

Mother and Father

sister

Grandfather

little
brother

cat

Grandmother

brother

dog

baby

Clothes

sweater

shorts

dress

boots

mittens

socks

hat

coat

shoes

At Home

house

chair

dustpan
and brush

table

lamp

clock

armchair

cupboard

key

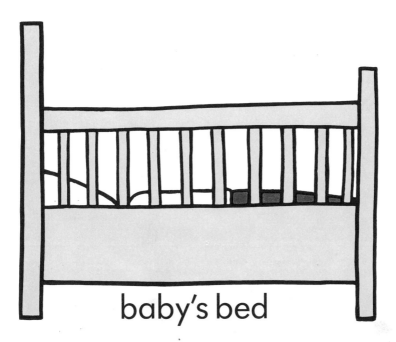

baby's bed

Toys

drum

teddy bear

puzzle

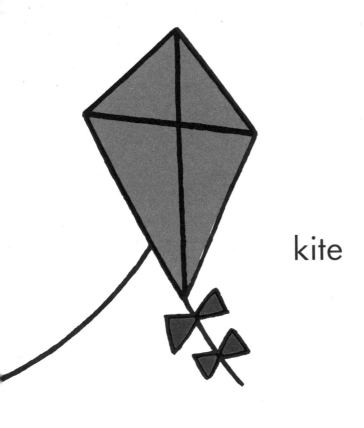

kite

engine

doll

trumpet

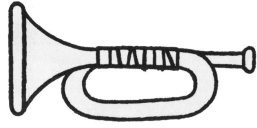

ball

At School

Class

scissors

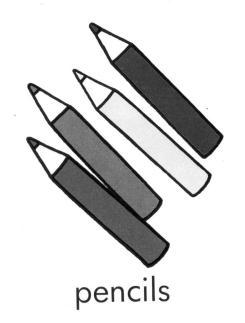

pencils

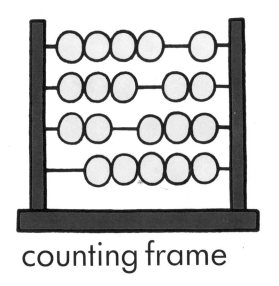

counting frame

xylophone

playing
the recorder

drinking milk

having lunch

playing soccer

reading

dressing-up

singing

Outside

flowers

bee

butterfly

eggs in a nest

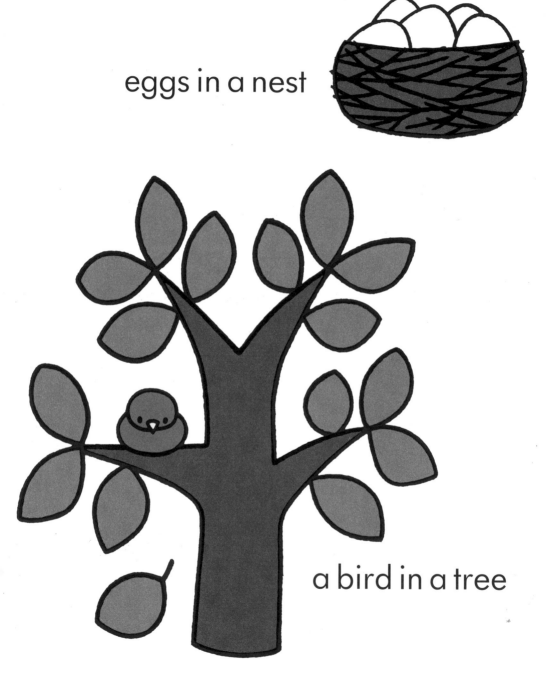

a bird in a tree

bird

snail

hedgehog

mushroom

People

sailor

fireman

nurse

doctor

policeman

skater

swimmer

skier

tennis player

soccer player

violin player

The Zoo

parrots

giraffes

crocodile

camel

penguins

hippopotamus

bear

tigers

elephant

lion

zebra

monkey

The Farm

farmer

farmer's wife

cow

hen

pig

cock

duckling

lamb

Which animals can you see?

First published in Great Britain 1982
by Methuen Children's Books Ltd
11 New Fetter Lane, London EC4P 4EE
Reprinted 1982 twice
Copyright © 1982 Methuen Children's Books Ltd
Illustrations Dick Bruna
Copyright © Mercis b.v. 1953, 1959, 1962,
1963, 1964, 1966, 1967, 1969, 1970, 1972,
1974, 1976, 1977, 1978, 1980
Printed in Great Britain by
Hazell Watson & Viney Ltd, Aylesbury, Bucks.
ISBN 0 416 21560 2